TURECK/BACH URTEXT SERIES

Critical and Performance Editions

Johann Sebastian Bach
Concerto in the Italian Style

BWV 971

Edited for Harpsichord or Piano

by

ROSALYN TURECK

G. SCHIRMER, Inc.

DISTRIBUTED BY

HAL•LEONARD® CORPORATION

7777 W. BLUEMOUND RD. P.O. BOX 13819 MILWAUKEE, WI 53213

I wish to acknowledge my thanks to Professor Christoph Wolff, Harvard University, for our discussions on the original sources and datings of the first two printings of the *Italian Concerto;* and to Professor Charles Jacobs, Queens College, City University of New York, and Professor George Buelow, Indiana University, for reading the Critical Notes for the first edition.

—Rosalyn Tureck

Credit to the editor must be printed in the program, or announced, when this edition is performed in part or in its entirety, whether live, recorded, televised, radio broadcast or otherwise.

Recorded by Rosalyn Tureck on CBS Masterworks, Record no. M35822 (U.S.A. & Canada) 76899 (Europe) and on Classical Music, Inc. CD TROY009, Cassette, TROY009C

Reproductions of the facsimile used by courtesy of British Library, London.

Second Edition, with a revised introduction by Rosalyn Tureck
Ed. 3377
Reg. # 48225c

TABLE OF CONTENTS

THE MUSIC TEXT

PERFORMANCE

CRITICAL NOTES

I. Original Sources

A. Manuscripts, First and Second Printings, Bach's copy.

The Italian Concerto, one of the two compositions which make up Part 2 of the *Clavierübung*, was published together with the *Ouvertüre nach Französischer Art*. The original title, *Concerto nach Italienischen Gusto*, may be seen in the reproduction here of the title page. "Italian Concerto" is an abbreviated usage.

No autograph copy of the Italian Concerto has survived. Although several manuscripts in other hands are extant, the most reliable source is Bach's corrected copy of the first printing, in which he has inserted revisions in his *own* hand.

The first two printings were issued by the same publisher, Christoph Weigel, in 1735 and 1736. The printings and Bach's corrected copy, consulted for this edition, are in the British Library, London, Shelfmark K.8.g.21, Hirsch III, 38, K.8.g.7.

The following manuscripts have been examined in a comparative analysis of variants and for general research background:

- Berlin - Staatsbibliothek Preussischer Kulturbesitz
- Mus. ms. Bach P215, pp. 76-88
- Mus. ms. Bach P295, pp. 288-296
- Boston, Mass. Boston Public Library
- M. 200.12 #2 Joh. Chr. Oley

Additionally, comparative analysis of the first two printings and the above three manuscripts was made in order to check and evaluate their variants in the light of Bach's revisions and printer's errors. The manuscripts, as dependable sources for Bach's intentions, are of limited value. The first two appear to be *copied* from the printing, while the Oley manuscript is regarded by some as possibly antedating the publication. They are of interest here chiefly as comparative tools in checking how closely they adhere to Bach's own copy.

As a result of this comparative analysis, the editor brings to light a textual error in the first movement which appears in well-known 19th and 20th century editions, including the Neue Bach Ausgabe, 1977. At measures 13-14 the figure in the soprano had been altered in certain 19th and 20th century editions to match measures 175-176 in the closing ritornello, creating an unauthentic symmetry. Neither the manuscripts, the first or second printings nor Bach's own copy contain this alteration. The present edition restores the original figure. (see: The Music Text, VI. Editions - Departures from Original Sources)

In the second movement a new treatment of the embellishment is revealed; the omission in representative 19th and 20th century editions of an embellishment in the original sources, as well as the alteration of Bach's original stemming is noted and corrected. (see: Performance, I. Embellishment - Second movement)

The inestimable value of Bach's text is self evident, and it is a rare instance in the keyboard works of direct contact with the original textual *and* performance intentions of J. S. Bach; consequently it forms the basis for this edition which, besides being urtext, is also edited for performance on the piano or the harpsichord in accordance with all the original indications in Bach's corrected copy. The stem directions, which, in the editor's opinion are of prime importance, have been restored as faithfully as possible. This original source provides so valuable an overall understanding of 18th century music notation and Bach's performance intentions that it is reproduced here in its entirety (p. xiii) along with its handsome title page.

II. Embellishment Symbols

One of the chief areas of interest in Bach's copy is his addition of embellishment symbols. The editor retains Bach's style of notating symbols. The realization of all embellishment symbols is given by the *editor* in accordance with 18th century performance practice, printed in each case below the music text.

III. The Edition

The music text and the performance indications in this edition are modeled solely on Bach's copy and the original printings which he supervised. They are not derived, in any respect, from any other edition.

The first two printings, as well as the manuscripts, contain articulation, dynamic, and embellishment indications. These appear here in accordance solely with Bach's own copy; they form the model for all of the editor's additional performance indications. The method of distinguishing original notations from those of the editor has been arranged as simply as possible and is explained in each pertinent section.

It has long been the custom to present a "clean" score with urtext references, leaving the performer without any stylistic guidance. This procedure has: (1) rescued editions from erroneous music texts and anachronistic performance directions, and (2) has reflected scholarly research and orientation. The bare urtext editions give the performing musician and teacher contact with the work of scholars and with increasingly reliable note texts which provide a textual foundation upon which an authentic performance art may be developed.

However, the awareness of the performer and teacher in relation to urtext editions must now move forward. In the case of a large body of Bach's music, there is no original autograph manuscript; therefore, a true "urtext" does not exist. In these instances, the rare printings with which Bach was himself associated and in which we see revisions in his own hand constitute the most trustworthy original sources. For this edition, Bach's corrected copy provides the primary source.

In addition to current editing procedures, performance practices must now be introduced, for performers require an urtext edition which will contribute to stylistic performance as well. To ignore, as in some editions, the performance aspect of music composed some 250 years ago is to omit the indispensable joint function of composition and performance. Substantial data is now available concerning specific stylistic performance devices and practice; therefore, stylistic performance instructions may be included within the precinct of urtext editions as long as the original source remains clearly in view by way of editorial treatment.

Instrumental means of expression and clarification of the performance style that the music of another era represents form basic facets of study for performers, teachers, and students. They constitute complex areas of knowledge and understanding which emerge from and relate to performance alone. Ideally, the work of the scholar should be integrated with the experience of the artist. The complete fulfillment of so great an art as that of J. S. Bach must embrace all aspects of the mutually dependent relationship of composer-performer and historical-contemporary performance.

The present edition provides: (1) the most reliable source of music text - Bach's corrected copy; (2) its original models of articulation, dynamics, embellishment, and stemming; (3) historical performance practices applied to both harpsichord and piano; and (4) aid in live performance applications of the structural, historical, and instrumental factors involved in the study, interpretation, and performance of the music on either harpsichord or piano.

This edition of the Italian Concerto *integrates* the textual sources with Bach's own performance indications, based on Baroque performance practices for harpsichord. These practices, when combined with an uncompromising purity of Baroque style, considerations of the musical structure, and *a piano technique which suits the style of the structure,* have valid applications on the piano. (see: Performance VIII. - Bach on the Piano)

IV. Format of Edition

A. Performance Indications

The *original* usage of the terms "forte" and "piano" are retained. The *editor's suggestions* for dynamics are shown in letters: *f, p,* etc.

B. Embellishment

An (o) indicates original embellishments, as engraved or added in Bach's hand. Suitable *additional* embellishment conforming to 18th century practice, has been recommended by the editor and is shown without the (o).

C. Articulation Indications

The articulation indications in the original source employ the slur symbol of varying lengths and the single dot signifying staccato. The editor's added articulation and phrase shapes are *modeled entirely on these* and are shown in lines consisting of *short dashes* occasionally associated with single-note staccato indications. Recommended staccato *sections* are represented by the word "staccato" in order to avoid fussy editing marks and any possibility of confusion with source indications.

To ensure that original performance marks may not be confused with those of the editor, (o) signifies the original source—Bach's corrected copy.

D. Clefs

The modern usage of continuous bass and treble clefs is employed in place of the earlier custom of changing clefs. The original clef indications may be seen in the facsimile reproduction here of Bach's copy.

E. Stem Directions

Upon careful examination, the notation of stem directions emerges as a major consideration in the perception of part-writing, phrase shapes, and contrapuntal relationships. Their significance has been frequently neglected or ignored, and they have been modernized in 19th and 20th century editions, including the urtext edition of the Neue Bach Ausgabe. (see: VI. - Editions - Departures from Original Sources) A few modernizations are desirable for the contemporary eye, but only where they produce no stylistic distortion upon the motivic shapes and part-writing. (see: V. - Notation Style and Part-Writing) The editor has, therefore, adhered as closely as possible to Bach's stemming, preserving the significance of the intrinsic polyphonic image which the individual stemming in part-writing represents. The reproduction given in this edition of Bach's own copy, which forms the primary source, provides an opportunity to study all of the original notation and stem directions.

V. Notation Style and Part-writing

Styles of notation differ with every cultural era. Each represents, in fact mirrors, the structural and performance symbiosis of its time and conveys musical messages by means of specific visual symbols significant to the musician of its own period.

The eye of the musician in reading and writing music reflect the ear and current concept of musical structure. The multiple stem directions in the manuscripts and early printings reflect a polyphonically oriented musical culture. A very different musical orientation is reflected in the notation where a single beam connecting multiple notes are all stemmed in the *same* direction. Such a notation system is suited for music conceived primarily harmonically but is *not* well-suited for part-writing.

This urtext and performance edition returns to Bach's notation style in order to reproduce with historical accuracy that which he himself used and approved and to revive the authentic structural and stylistic perception embodied in the original notation.

VI. Editions - Departures from Original Sources

A. First Movement - Mm. 13-14; mm. 175-176

Although the ritornello section (mm. 163-192) is identical with the opening section (mm. 1-30), it diverges in one significant detail. The figure at measures 13-14 is *not* the same as that in measures 175-176.

The original sources of the first two printings were published when Bach was fifty years old. His own copy of the first printing *agrees on the differentiation* between the figure in the opening and closing sections. In view of the fact that Bach was in a position to oversee the publication, this differentiation merits particular attention. The three manuscripts, cited on page i, also agree on this differentiation of the figure. Although it may be that all three were copied from one of the two printings, none of these sources introduced any variant in these measures.

Having compared the sources and found them to be unequivocally unanimous, the editor went further to ascertain whether there may be a structural motivation for this differentiation. The figure occurs frequently in the two rhythmicizations. Therefore, the question arises: Is there a structural logic in their nonconformity? The structural analysis brought the following to light:

The figure with the two thirty-second note values *preceding* the sixteenth as in its first entry at mm. 13-14, is employed *consistently;* the figure retains this form at measures 37, 38, 39, and 67, 68 as well. The figure with the two thirty-seconds *following* the sixteenth appears for the first time at measures 73, 74, then continues at measures 97, 98, 99, 100, and again at measures 153, 154, 155; and *is retained* on the return of the opening section at measures 175, 176.

The first figure never returns after measure 68. Altogether, the first figure appears *seven* times consecutively; the second figure appears *eleven* times consecutively. The picture could not be clearer: In the seven appearances of the figure in measures 1-68 only the first version is used; in the eleven appearances from measure 73 to the end of the movement only the second version is found. A da capo indication would have sufficed for the ritornello but the expensive procedure of re-engraving the opening section was chosen in order not to lose this structurally important variation. This discovery shows that the differentiation between the figures is not arbitrary, but rather, structurally essential to the figural relationship of the first and the second half of the movement.

The significance of this structural deployment was missed by the 19th century editors who arbitrarily "corrected" the figure of the exposition by bringing it into conformity with that of the ritornello. The effect, and no doubt the intention, was to create a conforming pattern in the opening and closing sections by imposing identical treatment upon them. But the very differentiation follows a structural logic, for the ritornello necessarily has a different contextual relationship to the whole than has the opening exposition. Moreover, the figure had already been changed to its second form at measures 73-74 well before the ritornello begins. The desire for identical symmetry is a relic from the concept of form emanating from the Classical era. The internal structural order of the first and second segments of the movement which involves this subtle, baroque differentiation, was canceled out by the editors who did not perceive it. They made the change by considering the appearance of these figures solely in the outer sections and deciding to match them. Further, the organic structure in the relationships of figural and rhythmic design of these two figures *within the entire movement* was destroyed. Initiated in the late 19th century, this alteration and its significance has gone unnoticed repeatedly, and the erroneous version is printed in urtext editions throughout the 20th century (see p. v). The correct figures are now returned in this edition to their rightful places.

B. Second Movement

1. Notation Style

The notation style of the original sources - the first two printings and Bach's own corrected copy of the first printing - retain the traditional polyphonic mode of stemming according to part-writing. The transfer of hand-written manuscripts to mechanically printed music did not change the multi-stemming notation style native to multi-voiced music. This is clearly visible in the printings of the period. However, some editors have chosen to change this style of stemming to the 19th century fashion of placing multiple notes on *one* stem connected to *one* beam. Although this notation style is more familiar to 20th century eyes, it destroys the polyphonic musical significance that multi-stemming preserves, for it represents *chordal* rather than *contrapuntal* structures. This edition restores the notation of the second movement to its correct notational depiction of a multi-part movement. (see: PERFORMANCE - I. Embellishment - Second Movement)

2. Measure 17

An embellishment ⋀⋀ is printed above the alto part on the third beat of measure 17 in the three original sources, including Bach's own copy. It is also present in the three manuscripts.

But 19th and 20th century editors have often omitted this embellishment symbol. Its presence directs attention to the fact that it is appropriate to apply embellishment to the alto part. The significance of this embellishment, as well as its inclusion per se in the alto part, has been unnoticed or ignored in numerous previous editions, urtext and otherwise. The analysis of the notational style in relation to the structure of the part-writing sheds light on the validity and the structural relationships that are fulfilled by the embellishment treatment in the middle part. (see: Performance - I. Embellishment - Second Movement)

Among those which have altered the original text and omitted the original embellishment are two representative 19th century editions and three 20th century urtext editions.

Alterations:

A) First movement ♩♩♩ to ♩♩♩
   mm. 13-14
B) Second movement, omission of ⋀⋀ in m. 17, 3rd beat, alto part.
C) Alteration of original stemming

Editions:

- B) Czerny, Griepenkerl, and Roitzsch - C.F. Peters, Klavierwerke von Johann Sebastian Bach, Series published 1868-1912, Italian Concerto, vol. 10, PN 8040. The alteration is reversed. Mm. 175 - 176 are altered to replicate the figure in mm. 13 - 14.
- A) Hans Bischoff, Steingraber - 1880
- A) B) C) Hans von Bülow, G. Schirmer, 1896
- A) B) Kurt Soldan, Edition Peters (Urtext) - 1937
- A) B) Rudolf Steglich, Henle Edition (Urtext) - 1962
- A) B) C) Walter Emery and Christopher Wolff, Neue Bach Ausgabe - (Urtext) 1977

PERFORMANCE

I. Embellishment

The recommended embellishment realizations in this edition by the editor are based on combined studies of treatises of theorists and composers of Bach's time too numerous to list here; the realizations are printed below the score.

A. First Movement Embellishment Symbols

The original embellishment symbols are clearly visible in this movement. (see facsimile reproduction.) These are retained throughout. In measures 47-48 the editor recommends the continuance of the embellishment, shown in measure 46, for the successively repeated figurations.

B. Second Movement

1. Notation Style and Part-writing

Throughout the movement, the *alto* part is notated consistently in the original printings, as well as in the manuscripts, with upward directed stems. These stems are connected to a single beam, signifying a single part. The *bass* part is connected to a *separate* beam. The two repeated bass notes represent a pedal point. They may be regarded as a fourth part, but only theoretically.

Continuous patterns of repeated notes—not isolated pairs—occur only occasionally in the multiple sonority structures in the Cantatas or, for instance, the organ works transcribed from Vivaldi and others. But this usage cannot be equated with the figuration here. If pressed into serving *solely* as an organ point, the two repeated notes, separated from the stepwise figure throughout the *entire* movement, become unrelated to the other parts, and, as a result, do not integrate into the total musical concept. Bach conceived his music in deeply integrated motives and related figures. Above all, the bass here is not a simple repetitive accompaniment. To conceive and perform the two repeated notes as a separate part will destroy the flow of the motivic eighths and create a repetitive, static figure that will stiffen the entire movement. Note the editor's recommended phrase shape in the score which *sustains* the line of the bass and the fingering which prevents a break in the line. Both contribute to maintaining continuity across the wide interval span. The cohesiveness of the part-writing is all-important and must take priority in concept and performance.

2. Motivic Structure

The alto part, one of the three meticulously notated parts, forms a separate motive, composed in a distinctive pattern.

3. Measure 17—Embellishment in Alto Part

Its ascending and descending line, its consistently regular rhythmic pattern and its structured, regularly spaced rests form a clear motive. The structure of the motive is amenable to embellishment and the set pattern invites the musician to add embellishment to this part. Measure 17 proves this point, for as noted above, the embellishment is added in the alto part on the third beat of m. 17 in every one of the sources - the manuscripts, the first two printings and Bach's own copy. (see facsimile reproduction of Bach's copy, Second Movement, p. XXV)

The editor observes the original embellishment in the alto part and bases the *rhythmic* placement of the added embellishment on that of measure 17, the third beat. Additional embellishment positions are placed on first beats when these strengthen and clarify the harmonic pattern as the soprano weaves its florid line.

Structural cohesion is strengthened as a result of the alto's emergence as a motivic part with embellishment, for it now functions in relation to the other parts—in particular, in imitation with the soprano part. The embellishment on the first note of the soprano part is familiar to all, but it has been isolated, unrelated to anything that precedes it in the three full measures before its entry. Now, the alto part receives an embellishment on the first down beat of each of the three introductory measures (mm. 1,2,3) as does the soprano on its entry on the opening downbeat of measure 4. The embellishment on the first note of the soprano entry relates to those established by the alto and *imitates* them. The balance of motivic entries is thereby established through the embellishment in *both* parts. A similar inter-relationship occurs at measures 28 and 29 when the alto embellishments in measure 29 on the first beat echo the soprano in its re-entry in measure 28, an *inversion* of the imitation at m. 4 in the opening of the movement.

mm. 1-4

mm. 28-29

The soprano part is a florid line. Note that embellishment symbols have been added to it in Bach's hand in his own copy. The embellishment in the alto part serves harmonic and rhythmic functions, leaving the melodic lyricism to the proper proprietorship of the top part. Additionally, the embellished alto motive frees itself from the bass part for which both bass and alto seem to rejoice. The bass and alto must at last, therefore, be accorded their rightful conception and treatment as distinct parts, each employing an individual motive. Performers will find it much more natural to play the lower parts expressively when conceived in this way throughout the movement. This is particularly true on the harpsichord where the embellishment is needed to impart fluidity to what is otherwise a static, repetitive pattern.

4. Stemming - Its influence on Performance

The alto embellishment in this edition will no doubt come as a surprise, since this part has been glued for so long and by so many to the bass, with both parts performed as though they were conceived solely harmonically, in the style of a double third accompaniment to a melody in the top line. This is a 19th century approach but, nevertheless, it has become ingrained in thought and performance throughout the last two centuries. As a consequence of this misdirected traditional view, many editions have altered the polyphonic stemming style of part-writing in Bach's own copy, the two printings and the manuscripts, all of which contain *identical* stemming.

The *two parts* have been transformed to double thirds; they appear on vertical stems, *all* in a single *downward* direction and connected together on a *single* beam. The original notation of individual stems connecting separate parts to separate beams, one directed upward, the other directed downward, is obliterated. The Neue Bach Ausgabe, 1977, has also departed from Bach's original notation in this way.

Bach's Copy

Neue Bach Ausgabe

2. Andante

The structural and the interpretive aspects of part-writing are thereby destroyed by creating, visually, a chordal accompanying figure of double-thirds. This notation style became established in the early 19th century, when harmonic concepts required the single connecting beam, uniquely fitting for chordal accompaniments. *Separate* stemming reflects the *multiple-voiced* structures of the polyphonic musical orientation. The single beaming in chordal style engenders a 19th-century sense of form and performance style. "Modernizing" notation does not serve the cause of authenticity, particularly because it represents a totally different style of musical thought and performance.

The added embellishment given by the editor is suitable for piano and harpsichord. The harpsichordist may add even more embellishment, but with great care, so as not to disturb the florid line of the soprano, which must retain its precedence in floridity and expressiveness above the lower parts. If additional embellishment is desired beyond that suggested by the editor, the harmonic, rhythmic, and voice-leading relationships to the other two parts which result from increased embellishment must be given full consideration before making definitive choices. Individual choices may indeed still operate if grounded in the fundamentals of the musical structure and historical performance practice.

C. Third Movement

No more than two embellishment symbols appear here in the original, and indeed the musical content of this movement does not require embellishment amplification. Arpeggiation of chords is desirable, particularly in cadences, and the last chord of this unmistakable virtuoso movement may justifiably be treated to a brilliant arpeggio and embellishment.

D. Embellishment Style

The realizations in the footnotes of the score are models for the rhythmic and intervallic treatment of each type of embellishment. The rhythmic treatment is to be followed closely but not mechanically. For instance, in the second movement, measure 17, the embellishments in soprano and alto parts, occurring in both hands simultaneously, form parallel fourths in the relationship of their first two notes. However, these need not be played precisely together; the slightest rhythmic freedom here contributes to the true charm of embellishment style and at the same time avoids the parallel fifths.

II. Arpeggio

A. General

Arpeggio was often implicit in Baroque and earlier performance practice. The arpeggio symbol, so much seen in 19th century music, is seldom encountered in Bach's work. The *word* "arpeggio" generally appears in conjunction with a series of chords. Couperin refers to arpeggio and its performance as "choses lutées,"* where chords are broken as in performance on the lute.

Chords on a solo instrument are often treated to some form of arpeggiation. Arpeggiated chords are a performing practice inherited from the lute. Fitting also to the plucked action of the harpsichord, this treatment is applicable and effective on the piano. The editor has recommended arpeggiation and added the arpeggio symbol in the score where it is appropriate for the stylistic performance of the chords.

---

* François Couperin *L'Art de Toucher le Clavecin*; Remarks, p.33 (Edition Breitkopf, 1933)

B. Rhythmic Applications on Harpsichord and Piano

The rhythmic and harmonic musical structure frequently requires the performer to employ on-the-beat arpeggio. Flexibility may be exercised in deciding the *time value* of the first note of the arpeggiated chord when performed *on* the beat.

1)  on-the-beat arpeggio: arpeggiate with strong accent on the lowest note, i.e., arpeggiate with low note played *first* on the beat and held in a longer time value followed by the remaining notes in shorter, equal time values.

2) off-the-beat arpeggio: arpeggiate with slight accent on top note, i.e., arpeggiate with top note played *last* on the beat and held in a longer time value than the preceding notes.

On the beat:

Off the beat:

III. Articulation

A. Original Indications

The original specific articulations which appear in the manuscripts, early printings, and in Bach's own corrected copy of the Italian Concerto prove the historical employment of *precisely planned* shaping of phrases in *slurs* of different lengths, often in combination with *staccato*. This evidence contradicts the assumption, often encountered, that Bach's music should be performed in continuous and undifferentiated detached touch. The first movement shows frequent original indications: in measures 15-20, 36-38, 43-45, 40-50, 61-64, 69-72, 75-80, and 177-82. These are:

The editor's articulation patterns are based upon these original models, and the editor's recommended phrase-shapes are notated in dashes ╱ ▬ ▬ ╲ . Original slurs are notated ⌒ . Alternative articulation is possible in some cases because of the multiple structural implications which so enrich Bach's music. Alternatives given for individual choices are marked by "or" in the score.

B. Harpsichord and Piano

The same general articulation and fingering directions apply to both instruments in the first and third movements, except in details. For instance, in the first movement, the editor favors the slur pattern, shown as alternative articulation, for harpsichord performance.

C. General

The long phrasing indications do not imply legato; they indicate the structural breathing points.

Consistency of phrasing-shapes is generally desirable and should be maintained, as original sources show, viz. First movement, measures 14-20, 35-36, 43-45, etc. Where original phrasing indications are lacking, the editor has recommended articulation possibilities. These include alternative choices at times: the preferred phrase shapes, once selected, should be retained in *all* corresponding passages.

D. Second Movement - Piano

Touch and Fingering in Part-Playing

Touch

For performance of this movement on the piano, the paramount requirement for the touch for both hands is legato and sensitive tonal molding. As has been explained above, the parts for the left hand are not simple harmonic accompaniment but distinct parts and must be treated in linear legato style. The editor's fingering is planned for maximal legato.

Fingering

Fingering has been provided which builds legato and articulation of meaningful phrase shapes into the activity of the fingers. In the parts which are

played almost continuously with the left hand, the original cross-under style of Bach's fingering is employed,* a method of fingering quite different from that of 19th century keyboard style. It can easily be seen how advantageous it is for the fulfillment of Bach's musical intentions. This fingering style prevents the chordal pianistic treatment of double thirds and encourages linear plasticity of the parts which does not deny the harmonic richness but contributes contrapuntal levels to the movement of the motives on both the harpsichord and piano. The editor's double fingering on one note, particularly that preceding the leap in the bass, creates a finger legato of utmost importance to part-playing. This connection with the fingers obviates dependence on the anachronistic "pianistic" approach to pedaling.

IV. Pedal Applications

A. General

The piano pedals function here in a totally different way from the 19th and 20th century style of piano pedaling. Their employment requires a new technical skill which suits Bach's contrapuntal and harmonic structures; these are based in a sense of form virtually alien to conventional piano performance. All pedal indications are the recommendation of the editor.

B. First and Third Movements

The sustaining pedal is hardly required in the first and third movements. The soft pedal is employed in the *una corda* sections of the third movement.

C. Second Movement

Because pedaling is so great a problem for pianists in Bach performance, the most appropriate applications of the sustaining pedal for the second movement where the greatest pedaling problems arise, are shown in meticulous detail by the editor. It is essential that the pianist observe the timing of the pedal precisely as shown by *p* and *x* in order to achieve harmonic clarity in the moving parts. The vertical dotted lines in measure 4 serve as a pre-

---

* see: *Introduction to the Performance of Bach,* Book I, page 12. Rosalyn Tureck (Oxford University Press, 1960)

cise model for coordinating the fingers and the timing of *p* and *x* to be employed throughout the movement. This pedaling technique—sparse, shortly spaced, with very swift changes—requires a fresh mental and physical coordination of finger and pedal skills, departing from standard pianistic pedal style. Its usage preserves the integrity of Bach's multiple structures.

V. Dynamics

A. Harpsichord Registration

The original "forte" and "piano" markings indicate manual changes for the harpsichord, from the louder to the softer manual. The harpsichordist is advised to follow precisely the original indications in all three movements. *mf, mp, p* apply only to piano performance.

Registration changes are not desirable within the "forte" and "piano" indications.

B. Piano

The piano style indicated here differs fundamentally from the conventional 19th and 20th century tonal approach to the instrument

No changes are made by the editor to accommodate conventional "pianistic" performance such as frequent crescendo and diminuendo; such changes belong to 19th century pianism. *f, p,* as well as *mf, mp, p,* are added by the editor only where they are considered advantageous for the clarity of the musical structure and expression of the musical content, and where they complement the stylistic dynamic indications of "forte" and "piano". These dynamic changes, represented in the original sources by the words "forte" and "piano", should be observed equally by the pianist and the harpsichordist. The additional dynamic indications recommended by the editor are based on the music's structure, on historical instrumental practices, and the aesthetic orientation of Bach's time.

(1) First and Third Movements
The pianist should follow the dynamic instructions with the original abrupt changes and differentiation of "forte" and "piano."

(2) Second Movement
The original "piano" in the alto and bass and "forte" in the soprano is easily fulfilled in performance on the piano. However, allowances are made for the successful delineation of this beautiful lyrical movement which the piano's capacity for subtle tonal molding makes possible. This can be done without departing from the original musical structures or imparting an anachronistic style of piano playing. Note that no gradual crescendo or diminuendo in Romantic style is applied. Tonal *molding* within *one* dynamic level is sufficient for purposes of expressiveness.

VI. Tempo

The first two printings of 1735 and 1736 as well as Bach's copy and the Mus. mss..200.12 #2 (Oley) and P215 agree on "Andante" for the second movement and "Presto" for the third movement. The first movement receives no indication. The editor's metronomic indications suggest, rather than a rigid instruction, an *area* within which individuals may vary. The area of tempo does not alter radically from harpsichord to piano, if the musical architecture and style are to be preserved.

VII. Fingering

The fingering recommendations, based on Bach's practice of cross-over and cross-under fingering, are applicable to both harpsichord and piano. Examples: second movement, the bass line, mm. 5-6 etc.; third movement, left hand, mm. 1-2 etc., right hand, m. 47, mm. 57-58 etc.

VIII. Bach On The Piano

This edition presents a style of piano playing that returns Bach, when performed on the piano, to his rightful tonal framework and structural relationships. The articulations and dynamics follow, consistently, the indications from Bach's own copy. The supplemental indications are based on the original articulation and dynamic instructions and are recommended in order to retain the clarity of performance essential for part-writing and for the contrapuntal textures and the phrase shapes that Bach's structures demand. The fingering contributes to successful articulation of the phrase shapes whether performed in fast or slow tempos with legato or staccato touch.

In addition to historical research and adherence to the most authentic textual sources, the editor's researches in period instruments, combined with performance experience on both period and contemporary instruments, form a necessary adjunct to editing for performance. The performance indications are directed to specific applications of historical, instrumental, and aesthetic performance style and *realistic* contemporary performance problems. The goal of this edition is to include not only the requisite scholarship for historical validity but also to reach beyond into the living realm of the artist and to develop and establish for the interpreter an authentic dynamic and structural framework for performance. It is also intended as a guide for the teacher and student toward well-grounded requirements for the valid expression of Bach's great compositional art.

The fundamental question as to whether Bach knew the piano has been definitively answered by historical documentation in the form of a receipt for the sale of a Silbermann piano to Count Branitzky. First brought to light in the Polish journal *Muzvka*, in 1967, this document contains the authenticated signature of Bach, dated May 1749, Leipzig, revealing that he was the piano salesman in this transaction.

The 19th and 20th centuries have provided numerous mistaken examples of 18th century concepts of musical form, structure and performance, often resulting in gross anachronisms. The virtuoso styles and tonal approach to the piano of these centuries, or attenuated dry purism, and their inapplicable sense of form and structure need no longer cast a shadow over the piano's suitability for stylistic Bach performance. From this edition one may see that the piano is capable of a new stylistic approach which suits the performance concepts native to the music. Fresh instrumental skills, original textual sources, and historical documentation may thus combine to establish an authentic kinship with Bach's vision.

FACSIMILE
EDITION

Zweyter Theil

der

Clavier Ubung

bestehend in

einem Concerto nach Italiænischen Gusto

und

einer Overture nach Französischer Art

vor ein

Clavicÿmbel mit zweyen

Manualen.

Denen Liebhabern zur Gemüths Ergötzung verfertiget

von

Johann Sebastian Bach

Hochfürstl: Saechß: Weißenfelß: Capellmeistern

und

Directore Chori Musici Lipsiensis

in Verlegung

Christoph Weigel Junioris

Reproduction of the Title Page of the 1736 Second Printing of Clavier Ubung—Book Two. (British Library, London; Shelfmark K.8.g.21.)

Reproduction of Bach's corrected copy of the 1735 First Edition. The original size is approximately 32.2 cm inner margin, 32.8 cm outer margin, by 23.0 cm at the top, 23.4 cm at the bottom. (British Library, London; Shelfmark K.8.g.7.)

forte
piano
forte

forte
piano

piano
forte
piano
forte

forte

6
Andante

7
Presto
forte

8
piano
forte
forte
piano
piano
forte

9
forte
piano
forte
piano
piano

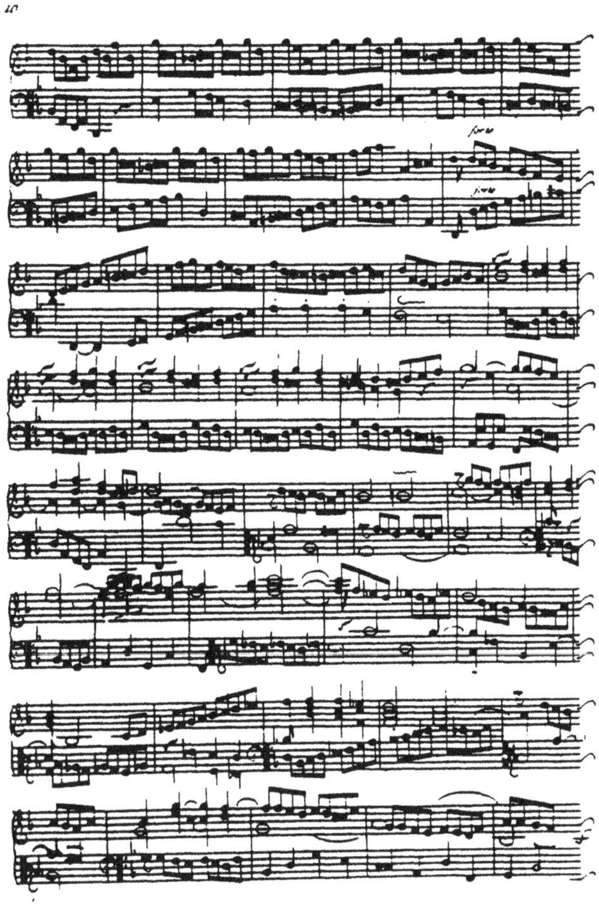

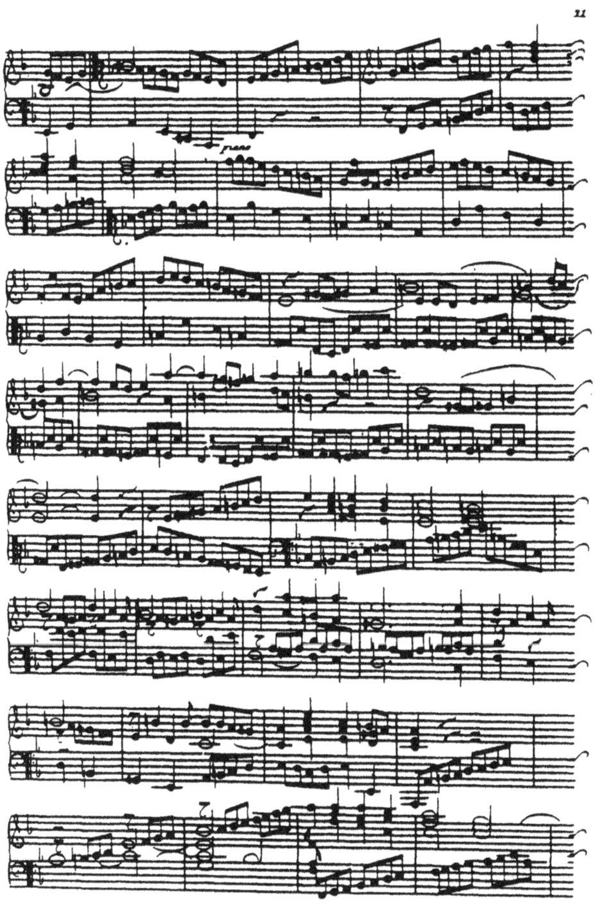

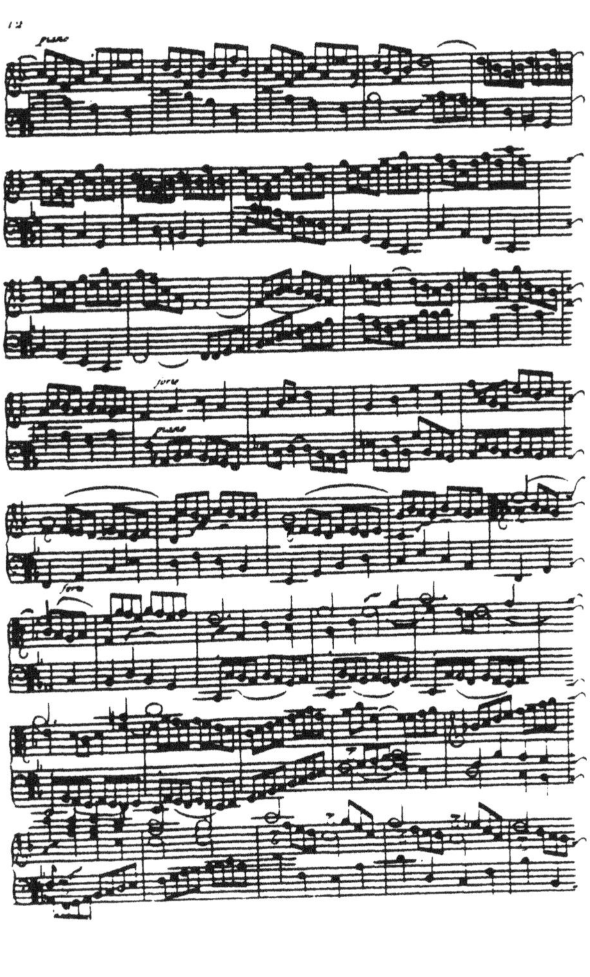

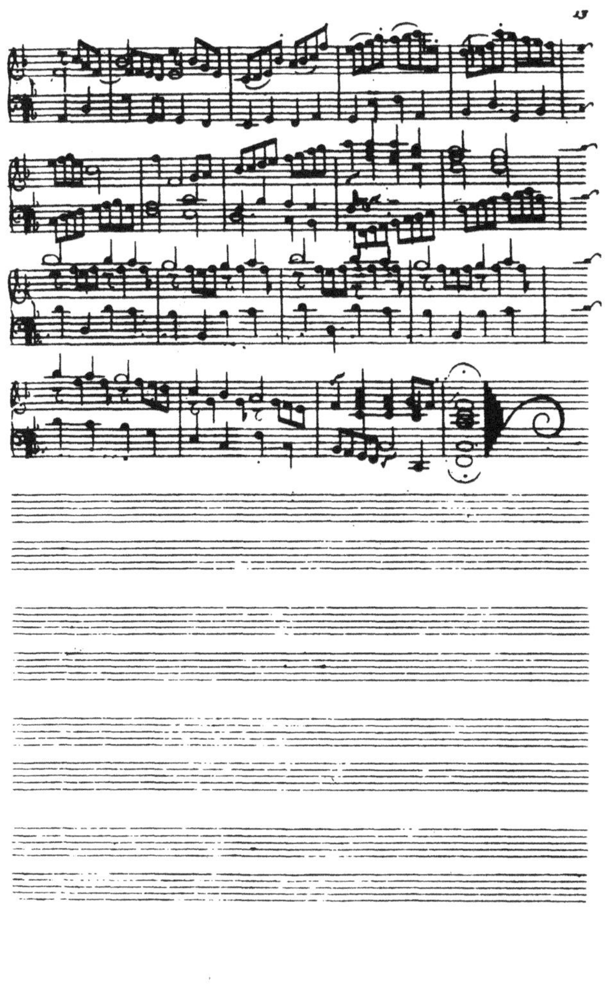

NEW CRITICAL
EDITION

Concerto in the Italian Style

BWV 971

Johann Sebastian Bach
Edited by Rosalyn Tureck

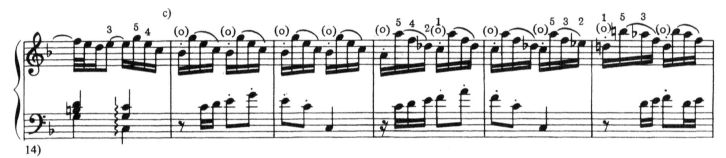

a) Arpeggio: 1) On beat { 2) Fore beat { All arpeggio indications are the editor's recommendations.

b) Nineteenth and Twentieth century editions have arbitrarily altered this figure to match the closing da capo section. The figure is now restored in this edition to the original version which agrees in all sources including Bach's own copy (see page iii).

c) (o) signifies original performance indications—articulation, dynamics, embellishments (see pp. ii-iii).

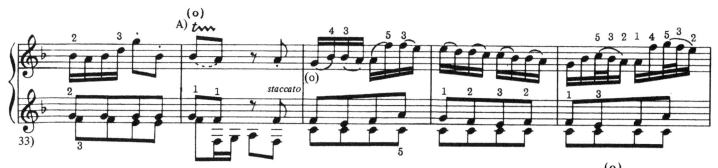

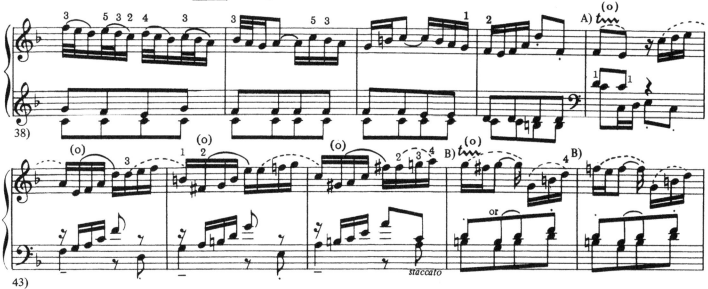

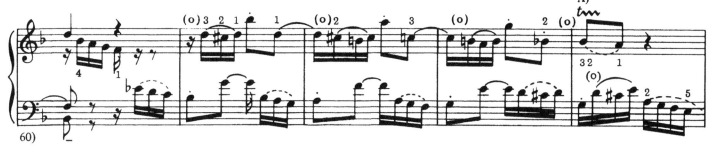

may be applied in mm. 47 and 48

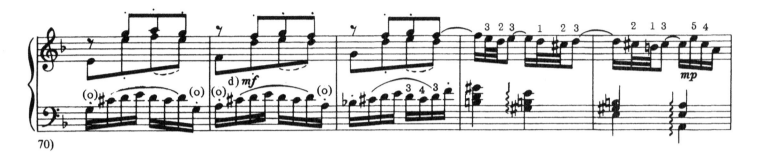

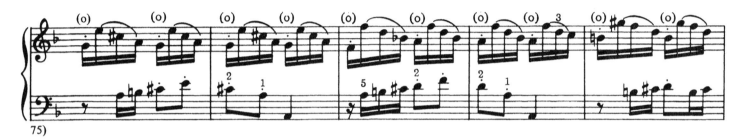

d) All **mf**, **mp**, **p**, apply solely to piano performance.

also mm. 93, 95, 149, and 151

96)

101)

107)

112)

117)

123)

129) *piano* *staccato*

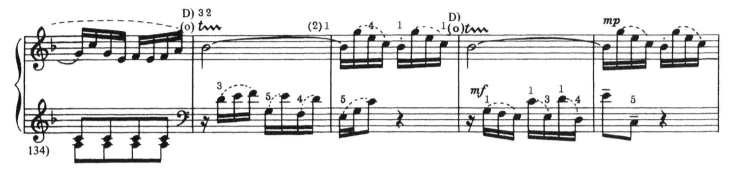

134)

139)

144)

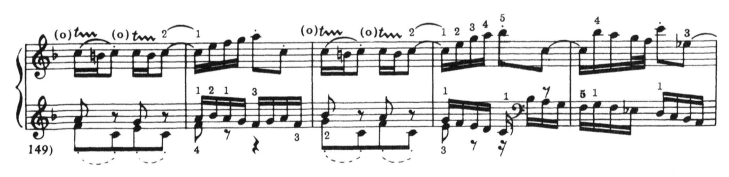

149)

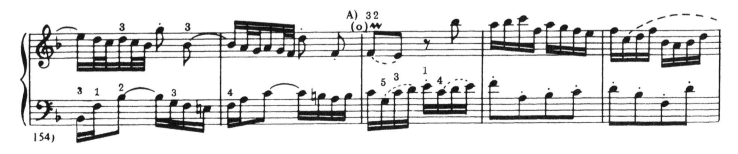

154)

159)

165)

172)

177)

182)

187)

8

NOTE:

All embellishments in the soprano part *and* the one in the alto at m. 17 appear in the original sources. Those added are the editor's, modelled chiefly after the original alto indication at m. 17 (see page v).

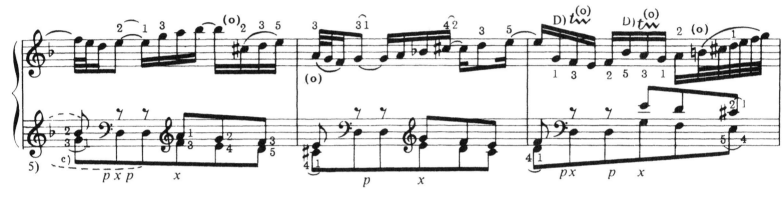

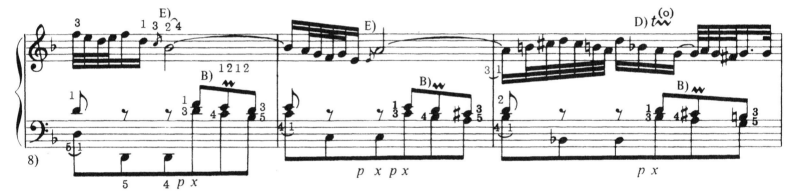

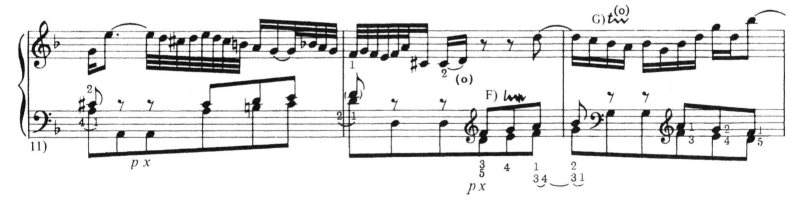

a) Phrasing remains same throughout in both lower parts.

b) Pedalling to be continued as indicated by *p x* and the vertical dotted lines in m. 4.

c) An easier fingering throughout is: $\begin{smallmatrix}1&2\\3&3&1\end{smallmatrix}$ but perfect legato is somewhat lessened thereby, in the lower part.

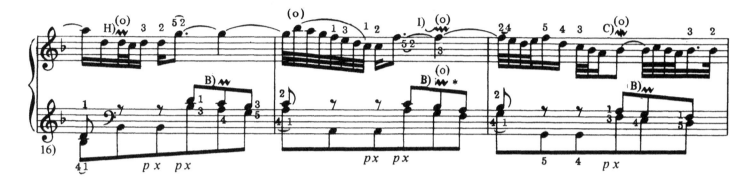

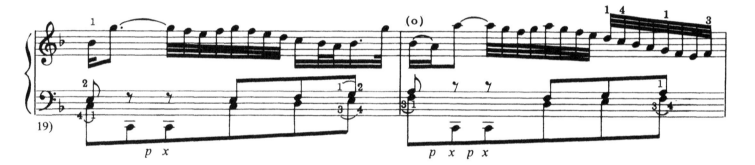

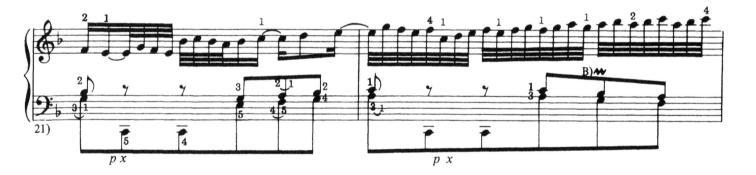

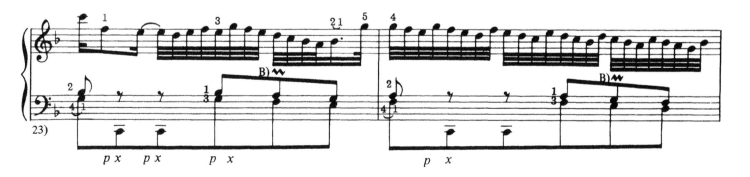

* see page.v, Embellishment—B) Second Movement.: "Found in all the original sources, the presence of this embellishment testifies to the fact that the middle part is an embellishable part."

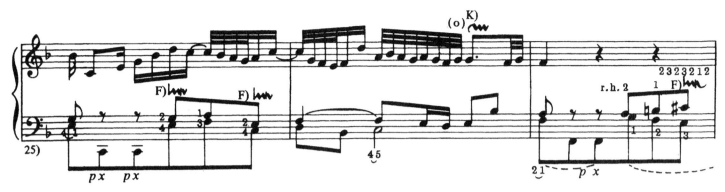

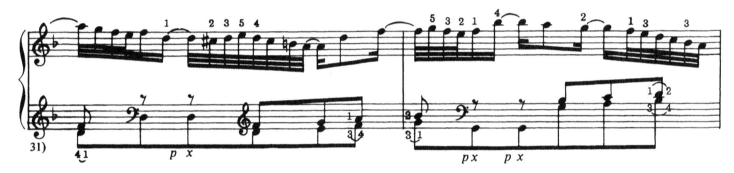

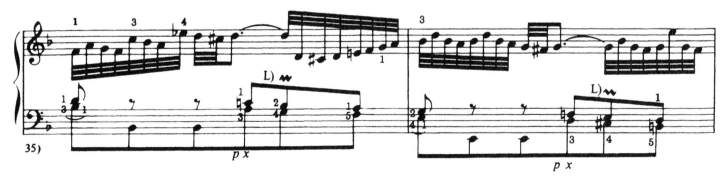

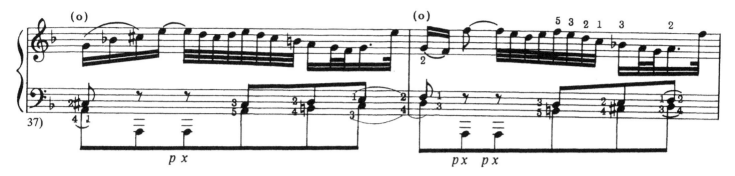

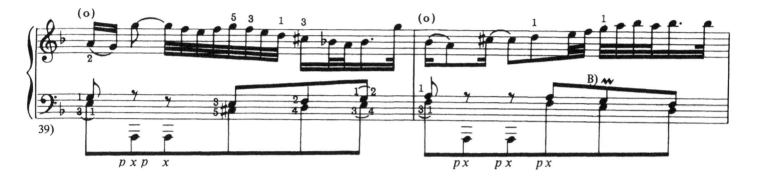

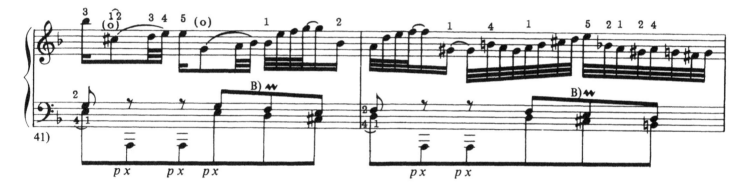

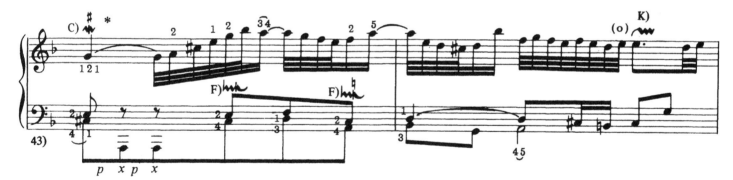

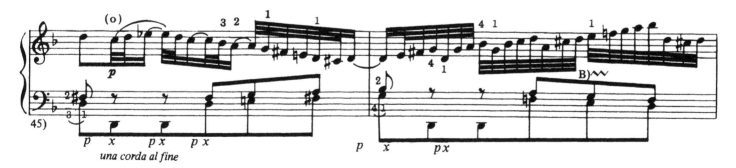

una corda al fine

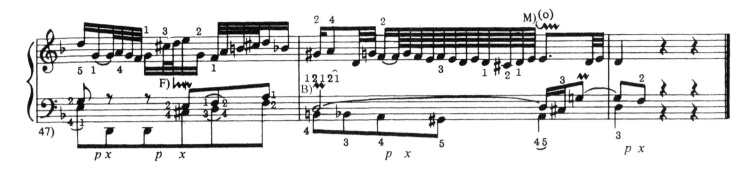

Presto $\quad \downarrow = 108 - 112$

M)

a[1]) The editor favors fingering employing the stronger fingers in the combination of 2, 3, 5 rather than 2, 3, 4 or 3, 4, 5.

a[2]) The use of the thumb guarantees the stress on the strong downbeat of the measure. This is required for the cadence, particularly since the following measure has no downbeat on beat one in the soprano part.

a[3]) See footnote a[2]) on page 2.

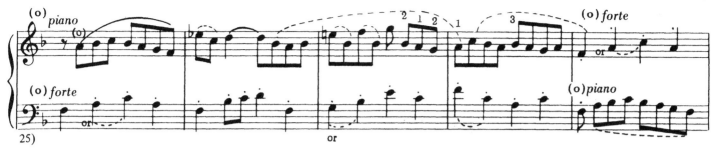

a) **Retain** staccato or slurred designs in each part throughout this section-mm. 77-91.

 a²) See footnote a²) on page 2.

c) Retain staccato or slurred design through mm. 155-165, and through mm. 175-180.

d) The position of 'forte' does not appear symmetrically in Bach's copy. See m. 53 where forte appears *on* the beat.

a²) See footnote a²) on page 2.